Strike Three, CHARLIE BROWN!

by Charles M. Schulz

Selected Cartoons from
BIG LEAGUE PEANUTS
Volume 1

FAWCETT CREST • NEW YORK

A Fawcett Crest Book
Published by Ballantine Books
Contents of Book: PEANUTS® Comic Strips by Charles M. Schulz
        Copyright © 1985, 1987 by United Feature Syndicate, Inc.

Library of Congress Catalog Card Number: 85-60951

ISBN 0-449-21290-4

This book comprises a portion of BIG LEAGUE PEANUTS and is reprinted by
arrangement with Henry Holt and Company.

Manufactured in the United States of America

First Ballantine Books Edition: May 1987

10 9 8 7 6 5 4 3 2

Strike Three,
CHARLIE
BROWN!

TODAY'S SPRING-TRAINING SESSION IS GOING TO BEGIN WITH A DEMONSTRATION...

LAST YEAR WE HIT INTO TOO MANY DOUBLE-PLAYS...

TWO OF OUR MEMBERS ARE GOING TO SHOW US HOW THIS CAN BE AVOIDED...

LINUS IS GOING TO BE THE SHORTSTOP, AND SNOOPY IS GOING TO BE THE RUNNER GOING FROM FIRST TO SECOND WHO BREAKS UP THE DOUBLE-PLAY...

NOW, WATCH CAREFULLY... THE PLAY BEGINS WITH LINUS FIELDING THE BALL, AND MAKING THE PLAY AT SECOND WHILE SNOOPY STREAKS TOWARD HIM..

AAUGH!!

ARE THERE ANY QUESTIONS?

SCHULZ

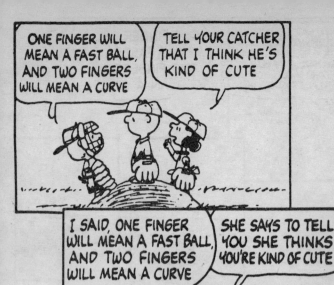

WHAT I'M LOOKING FOR IS A GOOD SHORTSTOP-SECOND BASE COMBINATION... TWO GUYS WHO CAN REALLY WORK THOSE DOUBLE-PLAYS...

WHAP!

CLOMP!

GOOD AFTERNOON...
MY NAME IS LUCY..

I'M GOING TO BE YOUR
RIGHT FIELDER... OUR
SPECIAL TODAY IS A
MISJUDGED FLY BALL

WE ALSO HAVE A NICE
BOBBLED GROUND BALL
AND AN EXCELLENT LATE
THROW TO THE INFIELD...

I'LL BE BACK IN
A MOMENT TO
TAKE YOUR ORDER

WHAT WAS THAT LAST PITCH YOU THREW, CHARLIE BROWN? THAT GUY MISSED IT A MILE!

THAT WAS THE OL' SCHMUCKLE BALL...LUCY INVENTED IT...

YOU JUST SORT OF SCHMUSH YOUR KNUCKLES AROUND THE BALL LIKE THIS AND THEN THROW IT AS HARD AS YOU CAN

EVERY TIME IT WORKS I GET A ROYALTY!

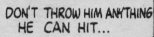

I'VE BEEN GOING OVER OUR TEAM RECORDS, CHARLIE BROWN...

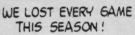

WE LOST EVERY GAME THIS SEASON!

MAYBE WE'RE BUILDING CHARACTER

HERE'S SOMETHING I THINK ABOUT QUITE OFTEN..

I'M SITTING IN THE STANDS AT THE BALL GAME, SEE...SUDDENLY A LINE DRIVE IS HIT MY WAY..EVERYBODY DUCKS, BUT I STICK UP MY HAND, AND MAKE A GREAT CATCH!

THE MANAGER OF THE HOME TEAM SEES ME AND YELLS, "SIGN THAT KID UP!"

HAVE YOU EVER HEARD OF ANYONE ELSE HAVING THAT DREAM?

ONLY ABOUT THIRTY BILLION OTHER KIDS!

EVERYBODY CAN GO HOME! IT LOOKS LIKE IT ISN'T GOING TO STOP RAINING...EVERYBODY CAN GO HOME!

IT'S HARD TO TELL EVERYBODY TO GO HOME WHEN NO ONE SHOWED UP!

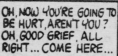

COME ON, CHARLIE BROWN, STRIKE HIM OUT!

I KNOW YOU LIKE LOTS OF CHATTER OUT THERE, MANAGER, BUT I CAN'T THINK OF ANYTHING TO CHATTER...

WELL, HOW ABOUT SAYING, "THROW IT BY 'IM, PITCHER," OR HOW ABOUT, "HE CAN'T HIT WHAT HE CAN'T SEE!"

ANOTHER GOOD ONE IS, "SHOW 'IM THE HIGH, HARD ONE!"

COULD YOU WRITE SOME OF THOSE DOWN? I'LL NEVER BE ABLE TO REMEMBER THEM OTHERWISE

THANK YOU... THIS WILL BE A BIG HELP..

"OKAY, PITCHER, THROW IT PAST HIM! HE CAN'T HIT WHAT HE CAN'T SEE!"

"PITCH HARD, CHARLIE BROWN!"

"STAY WITH 'IM, KID! YOU CAN DO IT, CHARLIE BROWN! BE GOOD BOY! GOOD SHOT! SHOW 'IM THE HIGH, HARD ONE.."

⚹ SIGH ⚹

HEY, MANAGER, I'VE JUST FOUND A SURE CURE FOR INSOMNIA..

PLAY RIGHT FIELD WHILE SOMEONE WHOSE NAME WE WON'T MENTION WALKS FIFTY BATTERS IN A ROW!

SHE'S PROBABLY BEING SARCASTIC, BUT THEN AGAIN, MAYBE SHE'S REALLY DISCOVERED SOMETHING..

I'VE NEVER BEEN SO HUMILIATED IN ALL MY LIFE!

WHEN MY TEAM RAN OUT ONTO THE FIELD, THE OTHER TEAM STARTED TO LAUGH..

THEY LAUGHED AND LAUGHED AND LAUGHED, AND THEN THEY ALL WENT HOME!

RATS!

POW!

CHASE IT YOURSELF! YOU WERE THE ONE WHO PITCHED IT!!

* SIGH *

HEY, KID! YOU WITH THE BASEBALL GLOVE! Y'WANNA PLAY RIGHT FIELD? WE'RE SHORT A PLAYER!

WELL, I'M ALREADY IN A..

Y'WANNA PLAY OR NOT? GET OUT THERE! WE'RE READY TO START!

I'LL BE INTERESTED IN SEEING HOW THIS LOOKS IN THE BOX SCORE...

YOU'RE THINKING TOO FAR AHEAD, CHARLIE BROWN...WHAT YOU NEED TO DO IS TO SET YOURSELF MORE IMMEDIATE GOALS...

IMMEDIATE GOALS?

YES

START WITH THIS NEXT INNING WHEN YOU GO OUT TO PITCH..

SEE IF YOU CAN WALK OUT TO THE MOUND WITHOUT FALLING DOWN!

IT'S A STRANGE FEELING WHEN YOU WALK UP ONTO THE MOUND FOR THE FIRST TIME EACH SPRING..

SORT OF GIVES YOU A FEELING OF POWER, EH, CHARLIE BROWN?

OH, NO, IT'S MORE A FEELING OF.... WELL, IT'S KIND OF HARD TO DESCRIBE..

I'D THINK IT WOULD BE A FEELING OF POWER..

NO, I THINK IT'S MORE A FEELING OF NEWNESS...AFTER ALL, IT'S A NEW SEASON AND A NEW BALL GAME...IT'S THAT KIND OF FEELING..

NOT POWER?

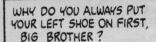

WHAT IN THE WORLD ARE YOU CARRYING IN YOUR GLOVE?

CRACKER SANDWICHES! YOU DON'T EXPECT ME TO STAND OUT THERE IN RIGHT FIELD AND **STARVE** TO DEATH, DO YOU?!

THERE'S NOTHING BETTER THAN TWO CRACKERS WITH BUTTER AND HONEY BETWEEN THEM

CHOMP CHOMP CHOMP MANAGERS JUST DON'T REALIZE THE PROBLEMS WE OUTFIELDERS FACE

CHOMP CHOMP CHOMP THEY DON'T REALIZE HOW BORING IT GETS OUT HERE WHEN NOBODY HITS THE...

HEY, PITCHER, I'M A REPORTER FOR THE SCHOOL PAPER...

WHAT DO YOU THINK ABOUT WHEN YOU'RE STANDING OUT HERE ON THE MUD PILE?

THE MUD PILE?

I'LL PUT DOWN THAT HE WAS A LONELY LOOKING FIGURE AS HE STOOD THERE ON THE MUD PILE...

THE MUD PILE?

HEY, MANAGER, HOW ARE THE ADVANCE TICKET SALES GOING?

WE SOLD ONE TICKET TO MY GRANDMOTHER

I SUPPOSE YOU'RE GOING TO PUT THAT IN YOUR COLUMN

WHY NOT?

" TICKET SALES ARE WAY UP OVER LAST YEAR "

"THIS REPORTER HAS NEVER INTERVIEWED A WORSE BASEBALL TEAM"

"THE MANAGER IS INEPT AND THE PLAYERS ARE HOPELESS"

"WE WILL SAY, HOWEVER, THAT THE CATCHER IS KIND OF CUTE, AND THE RIGHT FIELDER, WHO HAS DARK HAIR, IS VERY BEAUTIFUL"

GOOD ARTICLE, HUH?

WE'RE DOOMED!

DON'T SAY THAT!

OUR TEAM NEVER GIVES UP!

HOW CAN WE WIN? WE'RE TERRIBLE!

WE CAN WIN BECAUSE WE'VE GOT DETERMINATION

"KEEP A STIFF UPPER LIP" IS OUR MOTTO..

HOW'S THIS?

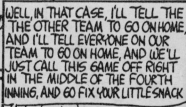

WELL, WE LOST THE FIRST GAME OF THE SEASON AGAIN!

I SHOULDN'T LET IT BOTHER ME, BUT IT DOES...

WE ALWAYS SEEM TO LOSE THE FIRST GAME OF THE SEASON AND THE LAST GAME OF THE SEASON..

AND ALL THE STUPID GAMES IN-BETWEEN!

STRIKE ONE!

STRIKE TWO!

STRIKE THREE!!

THAT WAS EASIER THAN TRYING TO REMEMBER ALL THOSE SIGNALS!

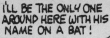

I'LL BE THE ONLY ONE AROUND HERE WITH HIS NAME ON A BAT!

THIS WILL REALLY IMPRESS THE KIDS ON THE OTHER TEAMS WE PLAY...THEY'LL BE AFRAID TO SEE ME STEP UP TO THE PLATE...THEY'LL THINK I'M A BIG-LEAGUER, AND I'LL...

HERE'S YOUR BAT, CHARLIE BROWN!

I HAD A LITTLE TROUBLE WITH THE WOOD-BURNING SET...

THIS BAT IS NO GOOD! IT'S TOO LIGHT! THAT BALL THEY'RE USING IS NO GOOD EITHER!

HOW CAN ANYBODY HIT WHEN THE SUN IS SO BRIGHT? I BAT BETTER WHEN IT'S CLOUDY! IT'S TOO DUSTY OUT THERE, TOO!

I CAN'T HIT WELL WHEN THE WIND IS BLOWING! THAT BAT I WAS USING IS TOO SHORT! IT'S HARD TO SEE THE BALL TODAY! YOU CAN'T HIT A BALL WHEN THE BAT IS TOO THIN! I THINK THEIR PITCHER IS..

GOOD GRIEF!